THE CHANGING

Littlemore
and Sandford

Jean Arnatt

Bob Crickmay

Carole Newbigging

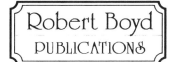
Robert Boyd
PUBLICATIONS

Published by
Robert Boyd Publications
260 Colwell Drive
Witney, Oxfordshire OX8 7LW

First published 1996

Copyright ©
Jean Arnatt
Bob Crickmay
Carole Newbigging

ISBN 1 899536 06 X

Anyone can publish a book!

Have you ever wanted to publish a book? It is not as difficult as you might think. The publisher of this book provides a service to individuals and organisations large and small.

Advice can be given on all facets of production: typesetting, layout, design and the processing of illustrations. Also the choices of paper stock, cover materials and finishes, binding styles including saddle-wire, perfect binding, sewn, limp and cased binding, the options are endless. If you have a project you would like to discuss why not contact:

Robert Boyd
PRINTING & PUBLISHING SERVICES
260 Colwell Drive
Witney, Oxfordshire OX8 7LW

Printed and bound in Great Britain at The Alden Press, Oxford

Contents

Cover illustrations

Front: Littlemore Old School

Back: King's Arms, Sandford

Acknowledgements

The contributors thank the Littlemore Local History Society, who kindly allowed unlimited use of their archives and all those who, in the past, donated material to the Society. Special mention must be made of the extensive research into Littlemore's history undertaken by the late Dennis Coombes, one time Chairman of the Society, and also of the work done by the late Tom White, a founder member, whose greatest wish was that a book on Littlemore be published. Grateful thanks to the members of The Littlemore Thursday Club and many other villagers for their invaluable help, particularly Jim Adams, Esme Hedge, Carol Jeffs and Audrey Willis, to Mr J Tanner and Mrs S Shatford for their contribution, and Joe Bewick for compiling the Littlemore Hospital section. The quotes used in the book are based on oral history recorded by the Littlemore Local History Society, and by Mrs Edith Feary.

Sandford material was, in the main, drawn from Bob Crickmay's own collection, but the contributors would like to thank the following individuals; Mr L Smith, Mr and Mrs D Harris, Mrs H Rowles, F Welch, Mrs Painter, Miss N Clack, Mrs Exon, Mrs Partridge, M Naish, Mr N Challenor, and C Langsbury.

Grateful thanks to Ms Chris Fenn for the sketch map of Littlemore and Sandford.

Walk about Zion, and go round about her, tell the towers thereof. Mark ye well her bulwarks, consider her palaces; that ye may tell it to the generations following.

Psalm 48, verse 13

Foreword

Littlemore and Sandford have always been close neighbours, priding themselves on their individuality, but sharing community activities and pulling together in times of stress, as witnessed during the war years. Both have perhaps been overshadowed by their industrial neighbour at Cowley, which provided much needed employment during this century, enabling Littlemore and Sandford to maintain their more rural way of life. The old way of life could not, of course, continue indefinitely, and progress is making rapid headway, with developments such as The Oxford Science Park.

Over forty years ago I took possession of a house on the new Minchery Farm Development. At that time there were no footpaths or street lighting, and St Nicholas Road was the only access. During this period the area has undergone the most dramatic changes, almost completely destroying our rural past. Old landmarks, such as the Littlemore Laundry and the old Vicarage disappeared to give way to housing in Marlborough Close and Vicarage Close. The open Sandford areas backing onto the Minchery Road became The Science Park and the Littlemore Hospital and Leys Clinic sites have been re-developed. Northfield Secondary and Littlemore Grammar Schools became Peers School, and housing development on the former Lawn Upton School land has robbed us of our only green space with wildlife, trees and plant life, because this was the only way to get the school modernised.

Sandford has not, perhaps, been so affected by modernisation, although the Sandford Link Road and Oxford Science Park were major changes to this area. The community can no longer rely on farming as its main livelihood. The paper mill has disappeared, following the fate of the Benfield & Loxley brickworks. Sandford is, however, still a haven of tranquillity and I hope it remains so for many years.

I am delighted that the history of these two areas is being recorded for future generations. I believe the photographs will give many people pleasant memories of what used to be. My wish is for the local community to flourish and I hope this book will enable the peoples of Sandford, Littlemore and Minchery Farm to appreciate the history of their area and the community spirit that is still very much alive

Councillor Joe C Blewitt JP
Lord Mayor of Oxford
29 February 1996

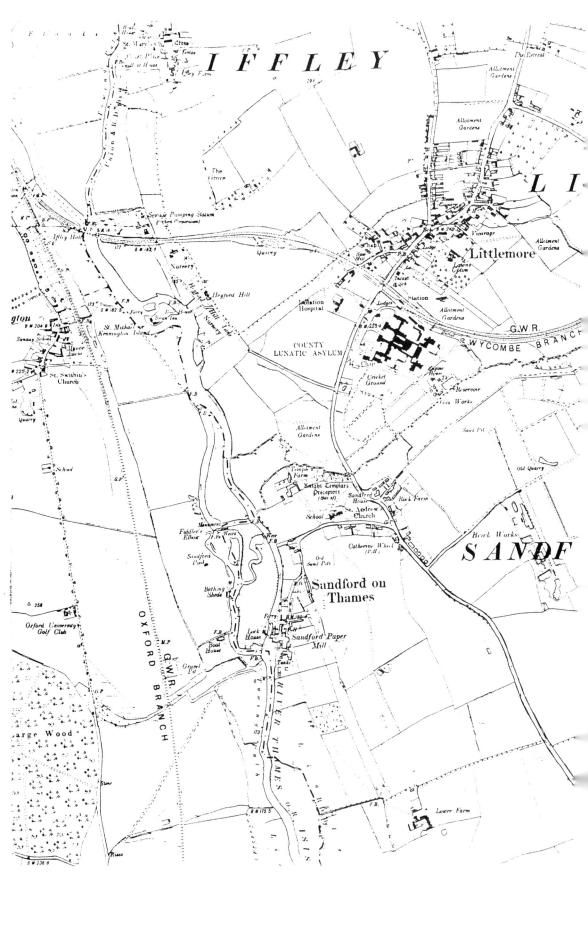

MAP
of the
LITTLEMORE
and
SANDFORD-ON-THAMES
AREA
circa 1922

Littlemore
and
Sandford-on-Thames

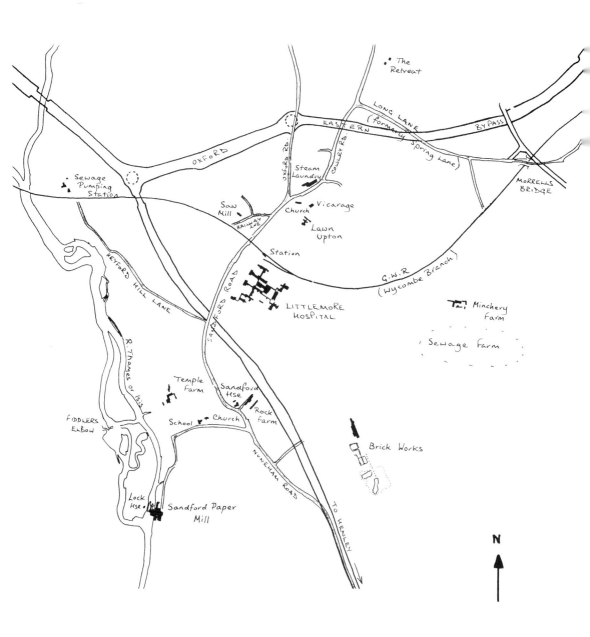

The Retreat

LONG LANE (formerly Spring Lane)

BY PASS

EASTERN

OXFORD

Oxford Rd

Cowley Rd.

MORRELLS BRIDGE

Sewage Pumping Station

Steam Laundry

Saw Mill

Vicarage

Church

RAILWAY LINE

Lawn Upton

Station

G.W.R (Wycombe Branch)

Minchery Farm

HEYFORD HILL LANE

SANDFORD ROAD

LITTLEMORE HOSPITAL

Sewage Farm

R. Thames or Isis

Temple Farm

Sandford Hse

Rock Farm

FIDDLERS ELBOW

School

Church

Brick Works

NUNEHAM ROAD

Lock Hse

Sandford Paper Mill

TO HENLEY

N

Original Road Layout

Around Littlemore

For many years Campion Cottage and the Manor House on the corner of Railway Lane and Sandford Road were one house, possibly dating from the 15th century. Campion Cottage, shown on the left with the door nearest to the road, is the oldest part of the building and in the 19th century, when a wall was removed, the original fireplace was revealed.

This row of cottages in Chapel Lane was built by Coopers, the ironmongers of Oxford, for their workers.

'There were nine cottages in the lane, then came the detached house belonging to Mr Nelmes, a foreman ganger on the railway. On the stone work of this house is the date 1774.' (Feary)

No 10 Chapel Lane, next to the Baptist Chapel.

Littlemore Baptist Chapel built in 1804.

On the opposite side of Chapel Lane stood these cottages, which bore the date 1820. Mr and Mrs Timms are standing outside the door of the first cottage. Mrs Elizabeth Bolt lived in the middle cottage. Mrs Hickman and her daughter Elsie, together with son-in-law, Edward Webb, are outside the last cottage, two other daughters, Grace and Margaret are by the garden gate. New houses were built in 1947 on the garden of this last cottage and the cottages themselves were demolished about three years later.

'Leah Timms used to make toffee and sometimes toffee apples, which she displayed in her tiny window and sell at a halfpenny each or two for halfpenny if the apples were small. Adjoining the Hickman's house was their well kept kitchen garden, then came the field, known as The Mere.' (Feary)

No. 2 Chapel Lane with Mrs Dean c1910.

'They were known as Spring Cottages, so called because of the spring which trickled from outside No 1 down towards the Chapel. The only water supply for Spring Cottages was from the pump outside the back door of No 1; it was believed that No 1 was built on the site of the original well. The pump was of iron and the sink was hewn stone. At the back of Spring Cottages was an access path known as 'the bricks' on the right hand side of the blue brick path going down to No 9 was a blue terra cotta gulley into which all household slops were emptied.' (Feary)

Shop in Railway Lane.

'The most important shop in the village was the Post Office and General Stores. This was kept by Mr Miller, the father of Albert Miller who later took over the business. Old Mr Miller was distinguishable by his long white beard and was often accompanied by a large collie called Rex.' (Feary)

The Grange stood near land now occupied by The Bungalow belonging to Mabel Prichard School, a school for disabled children. At the time of this photograph, c1908, it was owned by Miss Edith Allin, a member of a well-known Littlemore family, who took in paying guests. From 1934 to 1939 it was occupied by members of the Eade family, another well known local family. The Grange was finally demolished by Oxford City Council, when it was considered to be beyond repair, during the 1950s.

'At an annual parish meeting, someone reported the ghost of an old man on a tricycle having been seen on the new Minchery Farm Estate. The ghost was at once identified as Fred Eade. It is an understatement that nature had been unkind to Fred. Hunchbacked, his feet encased in heavy surgical boots, gnarled hands gripping a heavy walking stick and with an overhanging lower lip, he could hardly help being the best known figure in Littlemore. In addition his speech was difficult to understand until you knew him well. The most noticeable thing about it was the deep chuckle which seemed to rumble up from the depths as though Fred had some continual joke within him. He belonged to the Eade family which farmed Minchery from the City Corporation. He lived at the Grange, until it was demolished. (T White)

St George's, on the Cowley Road on the corner of Long Wall, was almost certainly built in 1611. Malting was a subsidiary occupation in the seventeenth century and there was a malt house at this property, when it was owned by Thomas Kimber. It was here that John Henry Newman lodged when it was owned by Farmer Giles, and the Rev Upton, Professor of Theology, lived here from 1914 to 1920. Through the double gates were two stables and a coach house and Mr and Mrs Symonds were employed as gardener cum groom and cook.

This view of Oxford Road shows Mount Pleasant in the background, a block of tenement buildings which is remembered by villagers as being rather a forbidding looking place. The buildings were demolished c1931. The present day Rose Hill roundabout now occupies the site. A field stretched from The Mount right down to the Cowley Road Littlemore, which later became allotments and eventually Cardinal House and Cardinal Close were built there. Families who occupied Mount Pleasant included Wicks, Kennets, Claptons, Jack Gardner, Fred Leach and Rowland.

Oxford Road, Littlemore in the early 1930s.   The boy with the cart is George Edgington.

Oxford Road looking towards the school with Dewes shop on the right hand side and Swinbourne Road on the left. On the left, just out of view, was the house occupied by District Nurse Lamborn and her brother, Edmund Lamborn, headmaster at East Oxford Council School, and affectionatly known as 'Ikey' by his pupils.

These thatched cottages stood on the corner of Long Lane and Cowley Road on what is now the site of Littlemore fish and chip shop, the existing row of terraced houses can just be seen behind.

The same cottages across the allotments in Newman Road. A hundred years ago Spring Lane stretched from Cowley Road, Littlemore to Morrell's Bridge, near the site of the present Blackbird Leys flyover. During the 1920s it was renamed Long Lane and the present Spring Lane took its name. In 1928 wooden buildings were built on the site of the cottages by Mr Clark, who used one as a general shop and lived in the other until about 1941. After remaining empty for some time the shop was later taken over by Zena Goodey. Behind the wooden building was Joe Hardings meadow where greyhound races were held. *'Long Lane isn't a long lane any more. They have blown up the old bridge and renamed part of the lane Sandy Lane West.'* (Welch)

Newman Road and, in the foreground, allotments on which has been built Cardinal House retirement home and houses.

Present day Spring Lane, known as Chowleswell Lane in 1605, after the Chawdwell spring near Northfield Brook. This brook was reputed to be good for bathing eyes, but with the coming of the sewage works the healing properties must have been destroyed. The land in the foreground is the present Nuffield Industrial Estate.

Cowley Road, Littlemore in the 1920s. The girls are standing at the entrance to Van Dieman's Lane and the row of chestnut trees still lead down to the house named The Retreat, a Victorian house built on earlier foundations. Local legend has it that Cromwell sheltered in its cellars during the Civil War.

Cottages on Giles Footpath opposite Charity Farm House. The first cottage was occupied for many years by Zena Goodey who ran a shop in the wooden building on the corner of Long Lane. In the foreground are the remains of allotment gardens belonging to the cottages in the background.

Adelaide House in Oxford Road, home of the Kempsons. This was originally two cottages and catered for cyclists staying overnight.

Broadfields was the house next to the Morrells Bridge and, until the car factory was built, there was an uninterrupted view of Shotover and Wheatley. Opposite the house was a 20 acre field which belonged to White's Farm in Cowley. In 1939 this was levelled for an airfield. Broadfields was home to the Welch family of small holders. Mr Welch was the Rate Collector, Clerk to the Parish Council, a Special Constable in the 1914 War and Trustee of the Alice Smith and Sarah Nowell Charities. He was responsible for two Overseers of the Poor, Mr Miles and Mr Avery. With help from his sons, their produce of vegetables and eggs was taken by horse and cart to the Iffley and Cowley Roads on Saturdays, using measures of bushels, peck, half peck and quartern until a change in the law required produce to be weighed and not measured.

The Village Hall.

In 1897 Miss Crawley gave land in Railway Lane for a Village Hall, stipulating that it was to be used exclusively by members of the Church of England, no political or sectarian meetings were to be held, and on no account was alcohol to be consumed or sold on the premises. Before building could commence a stone barn with a thatched roof had to be demolished. The money for the building was raised by the villagers and the builder, Mr Polly of Cowley, was paid daily until the money ran out. There were long periods when no money was forthcoming and during 1902–3 a willow tree grew in the shell of the building. Eventually, by holding whist drives in the Reading Room and a concert by the Black and White Minstrel Company from the Asylum, the roof was put on, but no money was available for windows. The outbreak of war in 1914 stopped building completely, but after the war each regiment was allocated a share of NAAFI profits and the soldiers from Littlemore gave their share to pay for windows. The Hall opened officially in the early 1920s. One of the dance bands which played here was The Crescent Four, so named because two of the members came from Crescent Road in Cowley. During the Second World War the Hall was used as a Civil Defence and First Aid Post and gas masks were issued. Mr Challis, a villager, gave lectures on First Aid, men on Tuesday evenings and women on Thursday evenings, stretcher bearers were trained and six or seven beds and medical instruments and boiling water were in readiness every night. After the war the Hall returned to normal use. However c1949, due to an explosion in population, it was called into use as a temporary classroom.

The house on Rose Island dates from Tudor times as a hostelry which later became a public house, called The Swan, catering for river trade. This ceased trading in 1926. The first mention of Rose Island was in 1618, the name is probably a corruption of 'red osier' which grew in abundance there. It was also known as St Michael's or Kennington Island. In 1889 it was sold to the Trustees of Mr and Mrs George Herbert Morrell's Marriage Settlement and in 1910 they leased a footpath to Heyford Hill Lane and a bridge was built connecting the Island to the Lane.

The original Queens Arms was a thatched Victoria building standing not far from the present one. The first landlord was W Davies in 1889.

The Golden Ball in College Lane was a coaching inn in 1605. In the 1920s, when Thomas Costar took over, the only means of lighting was gas lamps and candles, and Morrell's Brewery made improvements to the building and it became the first place in the village to have electricity. Stables at the back were made into a kitchen and bathroom and where the toilets are now was a store for 36 gallon barrels of beer.

The George in the Sandford Road would appear to date from 1766 and was a coaching inn with limited accommodation, stables at the rear and a nearby forge. Workers from the Asylum, coming home from the 7.30 p.m. to 6.00 a.m. shift, were able to call in for a drink, as the pub was open from 6.00 a.m. to midnight. In this view of Sandford Road, c1916, the two girls are standing outside The Old House, which dates from the 1700s.

Group outside the Old Marlborough on the Oxford Road c1930. Left to right: George Roberts, Bert Pullen, Jaffy Tanner, Bill Clark, Fred Pimm, Mrs Collins, Noel Kennet, Les Collings, Arthur Collings. Front row: Bob Adams, 'Rubub' Davies the landlord, Dick Davies, ?.

A Mr R Stimpson was licenced to sell beer at the Marlborough Head in 1753, but a public house is thought to date from before that time. The original building was on the Oxford Road. The name is from the Duke of Marlborough who held land in Littlemore. In 1937 a new public house was built at the junction of Oxford and Cowley Roads. This ceased trading and in 1986 the building was extended and converted into 16 flats and renamed Blewitt Court, after a long-serving Parish and District Councillor for the village who, in 1995, was Lord Mayor of Oxford.

The bus terminus was at Littlemore Church. The people waiting for the bus in this photograph of c1920 are from Sandford and had to walk from their village.

'The roads were made of flint and sand, dusty in summer and muddy in winter. The footpaths were gravel. The lighting consisted of two oil lamps, one at the church gate and one at the corner of Railway Lane. Later there was one on the Reading Room at the corner of College Lane.' (H Challis)

In earlier years, James Harding ran a carrier cart for passengers and goods to Oxford from Littlemore. An account given by his brother, Reg, stated that after the 1914 War he was discharged from the Army and with a gratuity he bought a horse and cart and set up a haulage business. Within a month not only did his wife die but also his horse. The Vicar, George Champion, organised a collection in the village and another horse was bought for him. After that he just concentrated on building up his business and his big break came when The Pressed Steel came to Cowley in 1926 and he secured a haulage contract there. The Nuffield Industrial Estate in occupies the site of his lorry yard.

Church and School

John Henry Newman was a Fellow of Oriel College, who later left the Church of England and became a Cardinal in the Roman Catholic Church. Whilst still at Oxford he became Vicar of St Mary the Virgin in Oxford in which parish lay Littlemore on land owned by Oriel College. He would often walk to the hamlet and became fond of its people and aware of their needs, one of which was a church of its own. However, he met with much opposition to this from the Provost of Oriel, who considered Littlemore too poor to support a pastor and also from the neighbouring parishes who stood to lose the double fees they could charge non-parishioners for baptisms, weddings, churching of women and funerals. Eventually, Oriel granted a piece of land and £100 and building work started on 16 July 1835.

The chapel consisted of only a nave with seating for 200 and cost £665 for all but the bell. No comment was made about the altar being of stone, which was illegal then, but some unease was voiced about a stone cross set above the altar perhaps being considered too Romanish.

The Bishop of Oxford consecrated the building on 22 September 1836. Because of its association with John Henry Newman, Littlemore is visited by people from many parts of the world.

Littlemore Church c1840.

The chancel and tower were added in 1848. Plans were made for a tower and spire but the spire had to be omitted as the structure was not strong enough to support it.

Littlemore Vicarage, demolished 1965. 'In 1964 negotiations were started to sell the Vicarage and build another house. The Vicarage was sold in 1965. Father Fletcher approved the plan and implicitly agreed the proposed site for the new Vicarage. But we could not sign the contract for this and a temporary house was obtained. The original house was sold for £17,500.' (PCC Minutes May 1971)

May Day party on the Vicarage Lawns 1933.

Newman's Cottages — The Reading Room.

In Newman's time, coaches and horses, as a means of transport, were beginning to be superseded by the railway, and he was able to purchase a range of buildings opposite and belonging to the Golden Ball. It consisted of a few cottages, stables and a barn, which he converted into his library and a place for contemplation for himself and like-minded students. Here he was received into the Roman Catholic Church and when he left Littlemore his friend, Charles Marriott, moved in with his printing presses. With local labour two or three books were printed. In turn, he left the buildings to the Oxford Diocese and it became almshouses administered for 100 years by the Vicars of Littlemore.

It became known as the Reading Room as newspapers, periodicals and books were available to villagers. In 1951 the Fathers of Birmingham Oratory bought the building and restored each apartment in 1958. The Old Reading Room is now a small museum of Newman memorabilia.

This photograph of 1936 shows the centenary celebrations of the building of Littlemore church.

The Church Choir at a service of Harvest Festival held in the Marlborough Head public house in September 1942. Clockwise from the vicar: The Rev C C L Buckwell in the background, Joyce Jones (nee Knights), Mrs Beckett and Dolly Phipps, 'Mousie' Goddard, ? Hodgkinson, Gordon Knights, Leonard Laitte, Roy Barlow, Peter Surman, Peter Wicks, Albert Bateman (landlord), Mrs Webb and Bob Miller.

A Church of England Temperance Society, certificate of merit, awarded to William Thomas Pulker, in 1905. The Society was established in Littlemore in November 1882, ten years later there were 106 adult and 63 juvenile members. The women used to meet at Lawn Upton House to make up bundles of clothing for distribution amongst the destitute women who had been rescued so that, properly clothed, they would be able to get employment.

The original Catholic Church next to The Shrubbery. A new Roman Catholic Church at Littlemore was built in September 1968 at a cost of £49,000. It was dedicated to Blessed Dominic Barberi, who received Newman into the Roman Catholic Church on 9 October 1845.

Littlemore School, known as The Old School, early 1900s looking towards Sandford.

The land for the school was bought for £25 from William Laffer by Newman and the school built in 1838. At one time Newman was worried about the state of the school as the teacher was lazy and he was afraid she drank. He recorded in a memorandum that the boys were ill-behaved and most of the girls were dirty and their hair had not been combed. A month later he wrote to his sister saying the girls' faces and hands were clean and he had put them to knitting stockings and was going to give them white pinafores for church, which they would make themselves.

May Day at Littlemore Infants School 1928. Left to right: Fred Fry, Joyce Smith, Jim Tanner, Eve Tanner, Eunice Slackton, Ann Bowler, Albert Almond, Mary Day, Raymond Strange, Louie Ching, George Clapton.

Littlemore School, rear elevation 1904.

In the 1900s the school consisted of a Babies Class and five standards, divided by screens. Between 1918 and 1920 the boys went to Headington School for lessons in metal work and carpentry. At first they had to walk, but later were taken by horse and cart by Joe Harding the local carrier.

School interior 1904.

In 1903 Mr Gibbs, the owner of Lawn Upton estate, offered a site for an infant school. The cost of the new building for 128 pupils was £1300 and by November £1050 had been collected by subscription, and the new school was opened in 1904.

Standard V from 1908. Left to right back row: Walters, Lee, Harding, Ovendon, Stevens, Shattock, Titcombe, Newman, Miss Anstey. Third row: Goody, Messenger, Partridge, Sylvester, Hall, Titcombe, ?, Foster, Barratt, Church. Second row: Clarke, Bradbury, Holton, Rowland, Bampton, Shattock, Baker, Clinkard, Withers, Clinkard. Front row: Cripps, Davis, Ireland, Challis, Fox, Smith, ?.

Littlemore School Standard I 1924. Left to right back row: Norman East, Reg Newman, Arthur Smith, George Schultz, Bill Barnett, Quartermain, Francis Leach. Third row: Rose Thompson, Phyllis Shermer, Marjorie and Mary Aishfield (twins), Phyllis 'Girlie' Pimm, Hilda Newman, Herbert Munday. Second row: Marjorie Baker, Daisy Fenn, Gladys Walker, Winifred Simmons, Grace Hickman, Mabel Saunders, Dorothy Haynes, Ollie Dixon. Front row: Tom Fry, George Newland, William Buckingham, Day.

A page from the school punishment book in 1911.

'In 1933 the school had become very overcrowded and a new school had been built in Temple Cowley so the older classes were transferred there. I then had to walk what seemed an incredibly long way to and from school. I had to become a dinner taking boy'. (Coombes)

Class late 1920s. Left to right back row: Edith Fry, Dorothy Dixon, Joan Tanner, Phyllis Newman, Alice Trafford, ?, Barbara Almond?, Florence Willcox, Marjory East, Dolly Tucker. Fourth row: Victor Strange, Douglass Moll, Laurence Bateman, Horace Smith, Raymond Mercer, Frank Saunders/Harding, Harry Coombs, Hiram Cordes, Ron Bradbury, Charles Buller, teacher unknown. Third row: Mary James, Ellen Barnett, Doris Seeney, Ellen(?) Phillips, Dollie Tanner, Vera Dewe, Nora Miles. Second row: ?, Welch, Ron Sewell, Bill Knights, Albert Strange, Christopher Whipp, George Day, Leslie Chamberlain, George Cracknel, Albert 'Jaffey' Tanner, Donald Miles. Front row: ?, Fred Silvester, Charlie Partridge, Reg Edgington, ?, Albert Reynolds.

Lawn Upton House.

In 1840 John Henry Newman purchased the land on which Lawn Upton House stands for £810 with the intention of building a monastic house for himself. However, in 1842, as he no longer needed the land he sold it to Charles Crawley for £726. Mr Crawley built a house in 1846 and lived there until 1881. It was later leased to Sir William Herschel, grandson of the astronomer, whose work with fingerprints led to their use in crime detection. After various tenants, the house was auctioned in 1919 and purchased by Thomas Carter. In 1929 it was purchased by Trust for the Sisters of Clewer and became known as St Mary's Home for Delinquent Girls. They left in 1948 and Oxfordshire County Council purchased the property and it became a school. The Crawley's crest is on an outside wall and, during Mr Lanham's time, permission to use the crest for the School was sought, and granted, from the Crawley family in Canada.

The Lodge.

Built at a later date than Lawn Upton House for the use of the groom. It is now home to the Headteacher of Emmanuel Christian School, who bought The Old School in 1995.

Mr Lanham was headmaster at Fringford School before coming to Littlemore. At that time there were 500 children on roll between the ages of 7 and 11 years. Some pupils came from Sandford and Horspath, and their parents had to agree that distance was no excuse for absence from school! At that time the cane was used but Mr Lanham felt that he had failed if he had to administer it as punishment. He was held in high regard by the children who still speak of going to Lanham's school. Mr and Mrs Lanham lived in Lawn Upton House.

Richard Lanham
Headmaster of Lawn Upton School
1938–1959.

Lawn Upton School staff. Left to right back row: Frank Tritton, Jack Walpole, Richard Lanham, headmaster, – Seaborn. Front row: Miss Morris, Mrs Davis, Miss Ruffey, deputy head, Mrs Hayes, Sylvia Colmer (later Mrs Tritton).

The parents of the children at Lawn Upton School raised money for a swimming pool. A committee was formed under the chairmanship of Richard Lanham, who, unfortunately, did not live long enough to see the opening of the new pool, which was dedicated to his memory. The inscription, chosen by his wife, reads 'May his peace be perfect'. Lanham Way near Speedwell School was also named after him. This photograph was taken at the unveiling of the plaque by Mrs Lanham and the Rev Young, vicar of Littlemore.

In 1988 the pool was filled in. The memorial tablet to Mr Lanham was moved to outside the main door of Lawn Upton House. The children no longer used the outdoor pool once Peers School pool was opened, and it had become neglected.

Littlemore Infant School Class I 1924. Left to right back row: Gordon Peters, E Day, F Bampton, E Sewell, O Bookham, E Wicks, E Walton. Middle row: Joe Welch, D Seeney, G Messenger, Albert Strange, O Phillips, D Barlow, A Trafford, L Champlin, T Adams, A Pannels. Front row: A Clark, D Tanner, D Barlow, ?, G Miles, E Walton, H Smith, O Dew. Teacher Miss Foster.

Littlemore Infant School 1930. Left to right back row: J Hall, M Peddell, J Knights, I Colbourn, I Pitson, P Shaddock. Third row: D Robinson, J Silvester, J Hudson, J Howell, M Quarterman, E Tanner. Second row: F Fry, D Titcombe, A Edgington, D Day, C Titcombe, R Sewell. Front row: F Burt, J Payne, B Howell, J Tanner, A Plasted, P Betney. Front desk: J Smith.

In 1956 a single wooden hut was built where present Florey building is. Later double wooden huts were built further down and used until the extension to Florey was built.

Speedwell Infants School c1970. Left to right back row: Mr Woodward, caretaker, Beryl Male, Jean Whitford, Ada McCabe, Maggie Devereux, Jane Kingston, Jean Walton, Enid Macey, Margaret Tack. Front row: Betty Storey, Kitty Ferriman, Jim Lynch, Chair of Governors, Marjorie Medhurst, headmistress, Mary Cowley, Susanne Keep.

The school was known as Littlemore Infants School until 1957, at which time the headmistress was Mrs Goodey. The name was changed to Speedwell Infants School, from 1957 to 1974, and then to Speedwell First School. Miss Medhurst was headmistress from 1957 to 1975. Soon after taking up her position as headmistress, Miss Medhurst applied for permission to change the name to Speedwell School, as the school grounds were covered with those plants. When it was granted, Mary Cowley, one of the teachers designed the School Badge which was made by Shepherd & Woodward in Oxford. The climbing frames, tree trunk and telegraph pole were installed on the playground about 1959. Miss Medhurst was also responsible for planting over 60 trees in the school grounds.

Peers School.

In 1938 Ron Ovenden of Oxford Road, Littlemore dug the first sod for the building of Littlemore Secondary School which, because of the wartime nature of building materials, was nicknamed Cardboard College. At that time the dark wooden buildings were also used as a rest centre and stored mattresses, kettles and other emergency items for the war years. The name changed to Northfield Secondary School, after the name of the brook that ran at the bottom of the school field. The permanent buildings of the first phase were completed in 1948, but, what were intended as temporary buildings, were not demolished until 1974. Mr Herring was headmaster from 1940, then Mr McGill from 1948 until his retirement in 1966.

In 1958 Littlemore Grammar School was started on an adjacent site, under headmaster, Mr Halliday. Later the two schools amalgamated to become Peers School, a comprehensive school named after Alderman Peers who was closely associated with schools in Littlemore. The first headmaster of Peers was Mr Bradshaw.

Mr McGill introduced the house system to Northfield: Windrush, Cherwell, Evenlode and Isis, which resulted in the school magazine being called Four Rivers. A similar house system was operated at Peers, under the names Hanover, Windsor, Tudor and Stuart.

Class 3A 1948, Northfield School.

Left to right back row: ? Bradford, David Titcombe, Stanley Bruce, Brian Deane, Peter Peverell, Donald Willmott, ?, Colin Smith, Keith Mills, Percy Collicutt, Peter Leaford. Middle row: Laurence Taylor, Anthony Mellor, Jean Sharr, ?, Sylvia Collett, Shirley Eden, Janice Bradford, Evelyn Barrett, Marian Steele, Susan Parker, Jean Hignell, Mary Lanham, Mary Barlow. Front row: Margaret Pratt, Sheila Foster, Moira McCockran, Miss Jones, Mr McGill, Mr J Evans?, Miss Orchard, Mr Shoduzsley, Barbara West, Elaine Cox, Jill Webb.

Teachers at Northfield School c1946.

Left to right back row: Webb, ?, ?, ?, Mrs Church, ?, Miss Spriggs, ?, Miss Clark, ?, Tom Hazel, ?. Front row: ?, ?, ?, Miss Donaldson the headmistress, Ted Herring the headmaster, Mary Orchard, Miss Ruffey, ?, Mr Colwell.

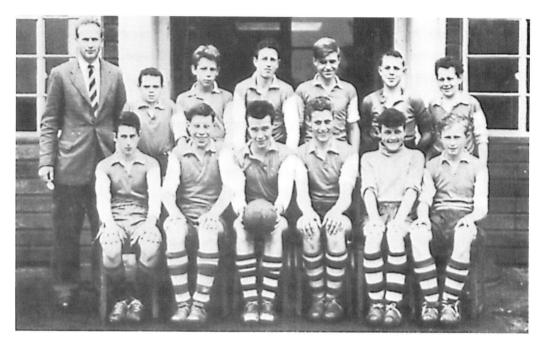

Northfield Boys Football 1st XI of 1954–55 season. Left to right back row: Mr J F Wightman, Michael Walsh, Michael Foster, Barry Dyke, Alec King, Alan Blockall, Randal Henwood. Front row: Peter Jackson, Michael Pym, David Kirkbride (capt), Morris Honey, Robert Parsler, Charles Smith.

Peers School Under 13 Hockey team 1971–72. Left to right back row: Lorraine Blewitt, Yvonne Sandalls, Elizabeth Dougan, Sandra Charles, Sheila Galloway, Wendy Tombs. Front row: Dawn Phelps, Nicola Cambray, Paula Hickman, Paula Cox, Hazel Adams.

SECTION THREE

Employment

Aerial view of the Hospital site 1952.

In 1843 thirteen acres of land were purchased to build a Lunatic Asylum for the County of Oxfordshire, which opened 1 August 1846 at a total cost of £29,286. During the first year 164 patients, 85 male and 79 female, were admitted, increasing to 234 by the second year and 347 by 1851, necessitating further building and expansion in 1852 and 1853 which included *'conversion of certain wards from being open plan to having side rooms, industrial shops and a wall for the coal yard, new baths and an extension to the ventilation and warming system.'*

Rules were drawn up in 1846 for *'the management of the Pauper Lunatic Asylum'* in 1846. These listed the duties of the management committee, regarding the inspection of the Asylum and the welfare of the inmates. *'Upon admission, he will be bathed, examined and clothed in asylum dress, and given proper attention and food.'* Visiting times were between the hours of 10.00 a.m. and 3.00 p.m. on Wednesdays and Saturdays, but inmates were not permitted to send or to receive letters unless they were first seen by the superintendent, *'but conversations between lunatics and their friends will not be prevented.'* The Housekeeper was instructed *'to employ as many as she can of the most trustworthy female lunatics in the domestic work of the chapel, offices and passages, instructing them and endeavouring to make it felt that such employment is a privilege. She may allow the best workers to dine with the servants in the kitchen.'* The male patients were occupied with shoemaking, tailoring and gardening, when the gardner was instructed *'to have such assistance as the lunatics can give, treating them with good temper and forbearance, not expecting from them such an amount of work that would entitle a labourer to his wages, not allowing them to approach each other in their work so as to interfere or to injure each other. He shall not use harsh language to them but to encourage them and to lead them on by kindness and friendly inducement rather than by compulsion'*

The Hospital had its own gas plant, fire station, mortuary, chapel and burial ground. Employed were the Clerk, Housekeeper, Head Male and Female Attendants, Head Female Laundry Attendants, seven male and seven female attendants (plus one male and one female night attendants), two laundry maids, fireman, shoemaker, seamstress, tailor, head and under gardeners, who all lived in. The Chaplain resided at the Dool House and a porter at The Lodge. Station Lodge was completed in 1866 as the house for the fireman, and in 1869 Brookside, formerly known as Gas House, was built as the cottage for the gas plant stoker. Littlemore House was built in 1883 for the resident medical superintendent, connected to the wards by a corridor.

The Hospital drew water from a series of wells, but by 1850 this proved insufficient. In 1853 the Oxford City Water Works offered to include the asylum in the water supplied from a proposed reservoir to be constructed on Iffley Hill, but this was too expensive and water was supplied from the brook flowing through the hospital grounds. This was satisfactory until the Local Board planned to flood this land with sewage under its proposed plans for the City of Oxford. In 1898 the hospital was finally connected to the City Water Works mains and the supply from the brook was abandoned.

In 1902 a further 35 acres were obtained to house another 200 patients, after the numbers had risen to 543. During the 1914–18 war the hospital did service as a war hospital and reopened in 1922 and became known as Littlemore Hospital. Staff houses were built in Heyford Hill Lane during the early 1920s. In 1928 a cinema projector was installed for the patients, later converted to give 'Talkies'.

The Hospital has suffered several fires; one broke out on Easter Monday 1895, when all the patients were taken to safety, but three firemen were injured and the roof and upper floor of the wing were gutted, and another in 1928 when the nurses' home burned down.

The Dool House was the house of Littlemore Hospital's Chaplain situated on the Sandford Road near the end of Heyford Hill Lane. It was also a nurses home and a residence for doctors. Built by a wheelwright, John Janaway, in about 1810 and purchased by Littlemore Hospital in 1848, it was destroyed when the Sandford Link Road was built and was replaced by a pair of bungalows constructed adjacent to the new road.

Male and female nursing staff 1904. After training and on successful completion of an examination, members of the nursing staff were awarded a medal with their name inscribed. This medal had to be worn on all occasions.

South wing after the fire on 15 April 1895, seen here from the cricket field.

Patients at Littlemore Asylum during World War I, when part of the hospital site was used for the medical treatment of soldiers.

Artisan staff c1890. Tradesmen would have included carpenters, shoemakers, upholsterer, tailors, blacksmith, plumbers and engineers. The workshops stood on the west side of the hospital, alongside the railway.

Albert Tedder's retirement from Littlemore Hospital c1964. Left to right back row: Tom Griffiths fire officer, Cecil Atkins painter, Freddy Grant joiner, Jim Adams joiner, Dave Tipton electrician, ? drainsman, Joe Coles, Gordon Goodgame fitter, Alfred Scraggs driver coalman, Bill Orger bricklayer. Middle row: Jim Duff storeman, patient, Stan Kirby joiner, Jack Sewell painter, Jack Gibbs fitter, Cecil Fox plumber, Les Allen electrician, Jack Blisset electrician. Front row: Eric Taylor electrician, Bernard Allen general foreman, Dennis Coombs engineer, Albert Tedder drainsman, Charles Wain chief engineer, Arthur Rose building officer, Bert Ringwald pipe fitter.

The Hospital Football Team c1925. Staff were not encouraged to play football to the same extent as cricket. If players were injured they had to continue on duty. It was not until 1953, when the hospital started to play league football, that it became popular among patients.

Hospital Fire Brigade 1953. Left to right: H Mathews, A Harper, P Corolenko, A Steward, J Bewick. The hospital fire officer, Horace Mathews, visited all wards and departments each day. He was also the hospital bookie.

The Laundry was formerly Linden House School, a private middle class school for boys. In 1871 the Schoolmaster was William Hurst. There were two assistant masters, Mr H Dickens and Mr R Hull, and seventy one pupils aged from ten to sixteen. Living in the house were also the schoolmaster's family, a cook, two female servants, a kitchen maid, nursemaid and bootblack. This photograph shows the school's letterhead.

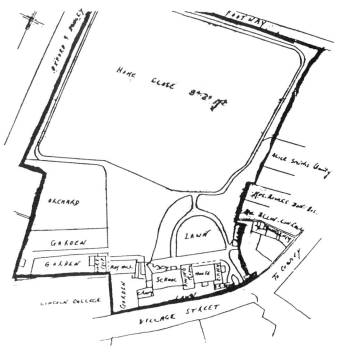

Plan of Linden House School.

Sundial House on left of Cowley Road, Littlemore. This was formerly the sanatorium for Linden House School. Newman's College can be seen on the right.

'The Oxford Sanitary Steam Laundry Company Limited have acquired Linden House, together with the school buildings and ground within the site at Littlemore and lately in the possession of Mr Hurst. The company are vigorously pushing forward the alterations and additions required for the present building and which, when finished, will be one of the finest laundries in England, having an area of over 102,000 square feet available for work... The machines to be used are those known as E Taylor's Patent Hexagon Eccentric, which washes the clothes in the simplest possible manner. All the steam and water pipes and fittings will be of copper and brass, which will make it impossible for any articles to become stained with iron mould... When in full work the Laundry will employ about 70 workers and will be capable of efficiently washing about 7000 articles per week.' (Jackson's Oxford Journal, October 1886)

Staff at the Laundry c1900. At this time the horse drawn van drivers were J Jordan, G Tanner and O East. Mr Wrenshaw was manager.

A laundry delivery cart, with the driver Mr Jordan. Littlemore Laundry did a lot of work for the Oxford colleges and many large houses in the surrounding districts. The bulk of the work was done by women, although the laundry employed a few men for work in the boiler house and as drivers for the three horse drawn vans. Washing and ironing were done by machine whilst the polishing and frilling were done by hand. Carpet cleaning was a speciality.

The Laundry chimney, looking along Cowley Road.

The Laundry from St Nicholas Road, shortly before demolition in 1958.

Corpus Christi Farmhouse, Sandford Road. This farm appears on a map of 1605. The thatched outbuilding was used as a farm shop selling vegetables, fruit, eggs and chickens during the tenancy of Mr Miles. During their time there were ruins of thatched pigsties. A previous tenant was Johnny Martin, who played the organ in the village church, and Mrs Martin who ran the Sunday School.

Laburnum Farm was at the bottom of Railway Lane until it was burned down in 1951 by a spark from a train hitting the thatched roof. The Fire Brigade at the Hospital was phoned but they were all away at the Amateur Football Cup Final at Wembley.

Littlemore Sawmills stood near the manor house near the corner of Railway Lane, later moving to the other end of Railway Lane. It was owned by Mr Earp, then Mr Tinegate, who also owned the teashop by the Marlborough Head in Oxford Road, Littlemore, and finally Mr Powell. There was also a timber yard in what is now St Nicholas Road, where Italian Prisoners of War worked during the Second World War.

The Continental Casing Company was the proper title but was known by villagers as the Skin Factory, as sausage skins were made there. It was situated where the Spud Centre is now located on the Oxford Road. A Mr Schultz took over the Company in 1926, which continued trading until 1958.

Littlemore Station opened in 1864. Milk was brought in from farms at Nuneham Courtney, The Baldons, Sandford and the Minchery for the milk trains to London at 8.30 a.m. and 6.00 p.m. The station was also the centre for coal for private use, the Asylum, the Laundry, schools, farms, pubs and smithies. Two local coal merchants were Charles Beecham and Gilbert Morris. The first car from Morris Motors to a motor show was sent from Littlemore, being packed and padded with straw and approved by Billy Morris himself.

Littlemore Station staff c1921. Left to right: Mr Shepherd from Wheatley, Bob Sawyer boy porter, R Collett, H Challis. Seated: Mr Jacques, Station Master, and Mr Foster from London. The staff comprised the Station Master, three porters and a lad who worked a twelve hour day until the eight hour day came into force after 1918. Porters earned 17s 0d and the lad 10s 0d per week. The Station closed in 1963, the last train running on 6 January.

The Steam Engine, Maidstone, was bought new at Maidstone Agricultural Show and is shown here being driven across the junction of Oxford, Cowley and Sandford Roads in 1898, probably on its way to the Station for shipment to South Africa during the Boer War. The man standing is John Allen and the driver is George Garlick. The pub in the background is the Old Marlborough, which was first recorded in 1753. The Bakehouse and Tea Rooms are on the right hand side where Frank Whitlock, the baker, made dough cakes for 2d and also cooked dinners in the bread ovens for 2d.

There were three smithies in Littlemore, one by the George, one near what is now Fairlie Road and The Forge House, pictured here by the double doors, opposite the Queens Arms. This forge was part of the Alice Smith Charity Estate and closed in 1924. About 1937 Mr Hebborn, a member of a well known fairground amusement family, moved into the adjacent house when the forge was still in place.

This shop was on the corner of Long Wall, where it joined the Oxford Road, and was at one time a Post Office. During the 1970s it was run as a Greengrocery by Graham Miles, a member of an old Littlemore family. It has now reverted to a private house.

The shop on the Bridge, Sandford Road, was built in 1936 by Mr Deacon, the owner of the property. Together with his wife, Florrie, he ran it successfully as a general store until ill health forced him to retire. The shop was leased to Mr Rouse for about two years and was finally sold to Mr and Mrs Jewell, who, with the help of their family, carried on the business of a general store from 1961 until they retired in July 1985. The next owner demolished the building in 1985.

PRIVATE RESIDENTS.

Acott S. H. 28 Eastern av
Adams Hy. (Geo. 7 Heyford Hill lane
A'Hern Rd. L. Station ho. Garsington rd.
  (postal address Cowley)
Aldir Mrs. 3 Oxford rd
Anderson Miss, Rose Isle
Anderson Mrs. Wright- Manor ho. Oxford rd
Avery Chas. Herbt. The Bungalow, Cowley rd
Avery Herbt. The Laurols, Cowley rd
Baker Benj. Springfield, Spring la
Baker Jn. 24 Eastern av
Baker Miss Edith J. Ivydene, Oxford rd
Bampton Frank, Bridge villa, Oxford rd
Bampton Geo. K., Glenallan, Spring la
Bannister Leonard, 15 Eastern av
Baskerville Fras. G. 26 Eastern av
Beckley Fredk. Prenton, Oxford rd
Beecham Mrs. M., Coalville, Oxford rd
Betney Regnld. Holmewood, Oxford rd
Billing Christian Edwd. 19 Heyford Hill la
Boaster Rt. 16 Eastern av
Bond Fred, 2 Eastern av
Bourne Ray M.A. (assistant to the Pro-
  fessor of Forestry, Trinity college),
  The Cottage
Brain Fras. H. 20 Eastern av
Brooks Leslie. West view, Oxford rd
Brown Wm. W. 29 Eastern av
Buckland Cecil Alfd. 4 Heyford Hill lane
Burnet Fras. Alex. 12 Heyford Hill lane
Butler Chas. 33 Eastern av
Bye Alfd. 44 Eastern av
Challis Herbt. Fairlight, Oxford rd
Challis Jsph. Edgecliffe, Oxford rd
Champion Rev. Geo. James M.A. (vicar &
  hon.c.v.), The Vicarage
Church Frank, Cowley rd
Church Geo. Sundial ho. Cowley rd
Church Sydney, Addlestone, Oxford rd
Coombs Edwd. S. 5 Heyford Hill lane
Crawford Wltr. Elm cott. Oxford rd
Cullimore Chas. H. 1 Eastern av
Dandridge Arth. T. 11 Heyford Hill la
Day Philip, 41 Eastern av
Day Wm. David G. Denecot, Oxford rd
Deacon Albt. Hill view, Oxford rd
Drinkwater Arth., Penlea, Oxford rd
Duke Hy., Rosemount, Oxford rd
Eade Herbert James Miller, The Grange
Evans Wm. The Glen (letters through
  Sandford)
Ferguson Mrs. John, Kings Lea
Field Roland G., Navara, Oxford rd
Firbank Mrs. Heyford ho
Glasspoole S. T. Cowley rd
Godfrey Harry, 43 Eastern av
Good Thos. Saxty O.B.E. The Hospital
Green Regnld. Wm. 16 Heyford Hill la
Halfacree Ernest, 39 Eastern av
Hall Wm. Alex. Delvashal, Oxford rd
Harding Chas. Westleigh, Oxford rd
Hayes Wm. 31 Eastern av
Hedge Rt. Bridge ho. Oxford rd
Hedges Bertie G. 17 Eastern av
Herring Mrs. E. A. Durley, Oxford rd
Hignell Gilbt. Wm. 17 Heyford Hill la

Hill Capt. Jas. S. M.C., M.A., B.SC. St.
  George's, Cowley rd
Hill Wm. 4 Eastern av
Honeybun Norris Wm. 6 Heyford Hill la
Horn Fredk. Warren, 20 Heyford Hill la
Horne Edwin Wm. 5 Eastern av
Horne Joshua, 34 Eastern av
Horwood Jn. 9 Eastern av
Hudson Jn. Arth. 3 Heyford Hill la
Johnson Arth. Spring villa, Cowley rd
Johnson Chas. Albt. Bridge view Gar-
  sington rd. (letters through Cowley)
Jones Gwilym, The Hospital
Kear Wm. 8 Eastern av
Kearsey Augustin M. The Retreat, Cowley
  rd
Kemp Leslie, 7 Eastern av
Langridge Jn. 14 Heyford Hill la
Langton Ronald A. 13 Heyford Hill la
Lardner Rowland, 18 Eastern av
Linnell Wm. A. 35 Eastern av
McDougall Wm. Adam, 18 Heyford Hill la
Mander Percy, 11 Eastern av
Miles Levi, Laburnum cott. Oxford rd
Moll Wilfred, Wayside cott. Oxford rd
Moss Cyril. 23 Eastern av
Neller Arth. 15 Heyford Hill la
Newman Jsph. Long Wall
Ovenden Albt. Jesse, Yeatlea, Oxford rd
Palmer Kenneth, 14 Eastern av
Pallett Arth. L. 13 Eastern av
Parker Edwd. Chas. 9 Heyford Hill la
Parsons Chas. 3 Eastern av
Pearce Chas. 40 Eastern av
Ponting Philip Hy. 22 Eastern av
Powell C. R. 12 Eastern av
Ralls Wyndham, The Hospital
Rawlings Fredk. 30 Eastern av
Reynolds Jn. Hy. The Hospital
Roberts Wltr. The Bungalow, Spring la
Rushent Arth. 32 Eastern av
Sandall Wm. Jas. 10 Heyford Hill la
Saunders Wm. 38 Eastern av
Scott Miss, Kennington Island
Shergold Herbt. 10 Eastern av
Sims Arth. Alfd. 1 Heyford Hill la
Smith L. R., 2 Heyford Hill la
Smith Wm. Whinfrey, Hawley, Oxford rd
Sporle Rt. Wm., Sunnyhill, Oxford rd
Steele Wm. Hy. 8 Heyford Hill la
Stewart Fras. Melville M.B., B.ch. Arnish
Stockford Thos., Arden, Spring la
Tanner Rt. 27 Eastern av
Thomson Jas., Laburnum farm
Trafford Regnld. 6 Eastern av
Treadaway Frank, Rumley lo. Oxford rd
Tripp Wm. Cowley rd
Watson Miss, Irydene, Oxford rd
Weiland Miss, 42 Eastern av
Westell Aubrey, Raymont, Oxford rd
Winchester Geo. H. Rock villa, Oxford rd
Yates Jn. Wm. 36 Eastern av
Yoates Geo., Ragpuize, Garsington rd.
  (postal address Cowley)
Yoshimoto Tadasu, The Shrubbery

Extract from the 1934 Kelly's Directory for Littlemore. (Reed Information Systems)

People and Recreation

An outing from the Queens Arms to Southend c1950. Left to right back row: Ted Clark, Vic Castle, Bill Clark, Ivy Long, Dick Cadle, Bill Long, Lil Cadle, Miss Trafford, Miss Trafford, Roy Massell, Mrs White, Tony Preston, ?, Mrs Clark, Mrs Walton, Mrs Clark, Jack Marsdon, Harry Clark, Danny ?, Mrs Preston, Charlie Commes, Gwen Walton, Bert Ives. Front row: Bill Walton, Lynne Castle, Mrs Clark, Mrs Walton, Jim Tanner, Mr Walton, Dot ?, Mrs Marsdon, ?, ?.

The Cricket Club.

Anyone over the age of 16 could be a member on payment of 1s 0d (5p) yearly. In 1892 both the Silver and Gold Cups were won by the Littlemore team.

The following year, Sir William Herschel levelled a piece of ground in one of his fields for use during the summer, in the hope that a Cricket Club for boys over 14 could be organised. An Annual Supper was held in the Reading Room.

Local characters: left to right: Polly Gibbons and Ada Dean of Littlemore, and Mrs Dodgson and Mrs Middleton of Sandford.

The Littlemore Derby and Joan Club, left to right: Polly Gibbons, ?, Edie Kempson, W Crawford.

The Rev George Champion with the Village Cricket Team c1920s. Captain Hill, with moustache, is seated next to him. Behind Capt Hill is Mr Mallam.

1st Littlemore (Lone) Boy Scout Troop c1928. This troop was formed by School Master, Herman Munday and held its first meeting in 1925 in the Reading Room. The uniform was grey jerseys and orange scarves. Cyril Tibbetts succeeded Herman Munday as Scout Master in 1930 and the troop became the 28th Oxford (Littlemore) Scout Group, with its headquarters in Fairlie Road.

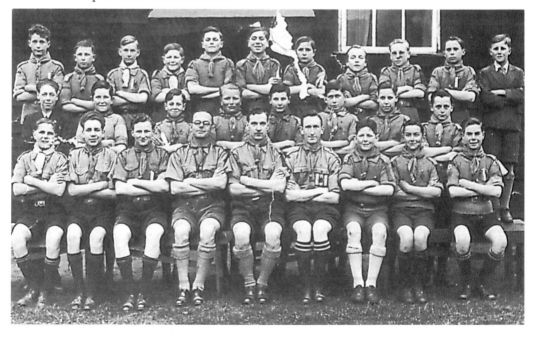

Scout group 1940s.

May Day c1934 on Oxford Road recreation ground. The May Queen was elected by the school children and the headmistress of the Infants School, Mrs Goodey, made the dress. There was dancing round the maypole, and the May Queen was taken round the village in an open top car. Left to right back row: Betty Shergold, − Beecham, Isabel Buckingham, Betty East the May Queen, − Smith, Queenie Wiggins, Joan Pollard, Ivy Clark, − Sly. Front row: Roy Wiggins, ?, Jim Adams, Lillian Partridge, Marjorie Beecham, Jim Lines, ?, Geoffrey Sells.

Littlemore School Football Team 1928/9 season. Left to right back row: Sydney Hale, Mr Tot Walton, Herman Munday, Harry Dean. Third row: ?, Buller, Baggy Lones, Walker, ?, Saunders, Kent. Second row: − Bradbury, Buller?, Simmons, ?. Front: Cuff Tanner, Tagg Walton.

The Hillsale Feast.

The Hillmanship land, was subject to flooding and consequently was of no use for agriculture and was leased to various farmers for use as pasture, bringing in an income of £3—£7 per annum. The land was situated in Heyford Hill Lane, opposite the entrance to Rose Island. The feast was held on Whit Mondays in the large Corporation Barn, which stood on the site of the Mabel Pritchard School, and the villagers paid 1s 0d for dinner and drinks when they took their own knives and forks. Prior to this the Committee Members and guests had lunch in the Reading Room so that they would be free to assist at the dinner. Any food left over was distributed on the following day to the poorest and most deserving parishioners.

The Feast was threatened in 1903 when Morrell's Trustees gave up the Hillsmanship land. However, the Committee collected funds and the local bakers, Mr Miller and Mr Walker, gave their help and the dinner was able to go ahead. After the meal, at 2.30 p.m. sports were held on the old Cow Ground lent by Mr Eade. The Asylum Band played in the afternoon.

In 1930 the Parish Council applied to the Charity Commissioners for permission to sell the land and it was eventually sold for £150 from which grants were made for children's sports.

This early photograph shows Kate Aishfield, in centre with hat, who lived in Chapel Lane.

Littlemore villagers on char-a-banc trip to Southsea c1930. Front row left to right: Bill Parker, Horace Saunders, Bill Knights, 'General' Walker, Bert Kent, Hilda Schultz, Mrs Wheatley?, Mrs Walker?, Isa Buckingham, Mrs Davis (Dolly), Daisy Grace. Second row: Mrs Knights, Molly Dixon?, Mrs Moll. At the very end Mrs Buckingham, Mrs Rose Crawford. Back row includes Hilda Wicks, Flo Matthews, Mrs Simmons.

Littlemore Football team of 1946–47 season, Oxford City Junior League Winners. Meetings were held in The George and games played on Oxford Road recreation ground. Left to right back row: G Harding, Jim Mercer, A Tedder, W Adams, Tom Jackson, Jim Adams, Malcolm Buller, Arthur Herbert, Bob Miller, Monty Matthews. Front row: Len Sharp, Ed Chambers, Jim Cox, Joe Fry, Pete Wheeler, Ernie Bedlow.

Littlemore Cycle Speedway Team (The Doddgers) c1945. Left to right back row: Colin Cook, Tony Hall, Bob Simmonds, Mervin Almond, John Dixon. Front row: Trevor Bostock, Ricky Whitworth, Tony Lapper, Terry Feary.

Speedway riders c1947, all local lads: Back row: Terry Feary, Brian Peters, Alan Clayton, Tony Lapper, ?. Front row: ?, Frank Johnson.

Mrs Annie Elizabeth Aishfield (née Hickman) came to Littlemore from Shutford in November 1902, after her marriage to Thomas Aishfield, a railway platelayer with Great Western Railway. Thomas died in 1917 and Annie was left to bring up three daughters, Mabel, the oldest, and twins Marjorie and Mary. She lived in Chapel Lane and Cowley Road, Littlemore, and later with her eldest daughter Mabel and her husband, James (Jim) Cooper, and her granddaughter Gillian at Long Lane, Littlemore. In 1949 she moved to Kempson Crescent where she lived, with Marjorie and Mary, until her death in June 1974. On 26 April 1974, Mrs Aishfield reached her 100th birthday, the first person in Littlemore to do so.

Edith Kempson was born 1894, the daughter of a male attendant and a nurse at the Hospital. Her father served 27 years at the Hospital, and became the first president of the hospital union. The family bought Adelaide House on the Oxford Road and the cottage next door, which they added to the house and catered for cyclists belonging to the Cycling Touring Club. Although the family were Church of England, friends of the family took Edith to the Baptist Sunday School, when she was about four years old. Thus began her long association with the Chapel in Littlemore, where, for 75 years, she was a teacher. In 1994, when the Parish Council, celebrated its Centenary Edith was the guest of honour as it was also her centenary.

PRIVATE RESIDENTS.

Allmond Fredk. 3 Nuneham rd
Beckett Chas. Nuneham rd
Beckett Mrs. J. Nuneham rd
Beckett Mrs. R. Nuneham rd
Beecham Fredk. Nuneham rd
Benfield Mrs. Sandford ho
Benwell Albt. 15 Nuneham rd
Bolt Arth. 1 Mill cotts
Boughton Geo. Jsph. 3 Mill cotts
Bullock Jn. Wm., High st
Challenor Mrs. Bassimer
Clapperton George Douglas, Mill house
Clapperton James Foulis, Elmslea
Clarke Alfd. Nuneham rd
Cornish Ernest, High st
Crickmay Wm. Nuneham rd
Dickinson Jn. 15 Mill cotts
Dive Clifton E. 8 Nuneham rd
Dodgson Harry, 13 Mill cotts
Evans Jas. Albt. Nuneham rd
Foster Cyril, Red cott
Fox Edwd. 5 Nuneham rd
Gaskell Matthew Wm. Burneside
Gibbons Frank, 10 Nuneham rd
Gomm Fras. Hy. The Croft, Nuneham rd
Harris Jn. The Mount, Nuneham rd
Harris Wltr. 9 Nuneham rd
Henderson Wm. Mill ho
Higgins Wm., Airdrie ho. Nuneham rd
Honey Geo., High st
Hooson-Parker Wm. F., The Bungalow
James Geo. Rd. 14 Nuneham rd
Kerrod Frank, Peacock cott
Langsbury Benj. 16 Mill cotts
Langsbury Mrs. 7 Mill cotts
Leach Fredk. 14 Mill cotts
Leach Jn. Wm. 12 Mill cotts
Leach Mrs. J. 8 Mill cotts
Matthews Fredk., Nuneham rd
Middleton Fredk., Nuneham rd
Middleton Jsph. Nuneham rd
Morris Edwd. Nuneham rd
Naish Chas., Nuneham rd
Naish Edwd., Albany ho. Nuneham rd
Naish Harry, 9 Mill cotts
Naish Mrs., Nuneham rd
Naish Percvl. 7 Nuneham rd
Naish Wltr Jas. 1 Nuneham rd
Naish Wm., Rock cotts

Osborne Percvl. 11 Nuneham rd
Partridge Mrs. Nuneham rd
Payne Hy. Nuneham rd
Petch Rt. Jn. Nuneham rd
Pittson Chas. Leonard, 2 Mill cotts
Reeve Fredk. Nuneham rd
Reeve Thos. 16 Nuneham rd
Rivers Wm 6 Nuneham rd
Saving David, 12 Nuneham rd
Sharp Chas. Nuneham rd
Sharp Rt. Nuneham rd
Shepherd Fredk. 13 Nuneham rd
Silvester Mrs., High st
Smith Wm. Hazel, 2 Nuneham rd
Stone Albt. High st
Stone Arth. 4 Nuneham rd
Taylor Fredk. 10 Mill cotts
Turner Wilfred, 4 Mill cotts
Tutty Albt. 5 Mill cotts
Vaughan Harry, Nuneham rd
Webb Mrs.. High st
White Fredk. Chas., High st
White Hy. High st
Windsor Gilbt. 6 Mill cotts

COMMERCIAL.

Anderson & Bucknall, electrcl. engnrs
Barrett Charles William, beer retailer
British Legion (Sandford branch) (Fredk. Reeve, sec)
Cannon & Clapperton (1926) Ltd. paper mfrs
Cooper George, boot repairer
Cornish Arth. farmer, Temple farm
Davis Jesse, police sergeant, County Police station
Eade Harry Hammond, farmer, Mynchery farm (postal address Littlemore)
Goldhawk Alfd. Thos. lock keeper
Herring Harry, parcel depot for omnibuses, Nuneham rd
Keene Wltr. Raymond B. farmer, Rock farm
King's Arms hotel (Mrs. F.K.Woodbridge)
Naish Ernest, baker, & post office
Rowles Geo. Arth. motor engnr. Nuneham rd
Stephens Albt. S. Catherine Wheel P.H
Tinson Leonard, constable, County Police station

Extract from the 1934 Kelly's Directory for Sandford. (Reed Information Systems)

Around Sandford on Thames

The London Road.

An ancient roadway from Oxford to Wallingford and London, formerly the Wallingford Way. This view of c1910 is taken from Fox Hill down the old London Road. The house at the far end is in Sandford Lane and here the road takes a sharp S bend before going on to Sandford Gate and the Toll House. The large house on the right is Sandford Farm House, an 18th century building. The lofty elms in the field on the left were felled for a new road cut through in 1931. The road was 'turnpiked' from Henley to Oxford in 1736.

Looking up the old London Road towards the Fox Public House, with the new 1931 road on the right. The grass verge between the two roads is a remnant of the old field named Church Close.

The original turnpike bridge c1927. To the left, behind the trees, can be seen The Glen built in 1921 which replaced the old Toll Keepers Cottage. When the turnpike trust ended in 1873 Sandford Toll House and gardens were valued at £48 15s.

The Glen pictured during the 1920s.

A row of outbuildings within the grounds of Sandford House, converted to cottages around the 1880s. At one time known as Bravington's Rookery.

Sandford House, a 17th century building, that once had extensive orchards, gardens and outbuildings. By 1880 some of the outbuildings had been converted to cottages and the servants quarters and dairy converted into two separate houses. This was home to Mr Benfield in the early 1900s.

Rock Farm Lane in the 1960s, looking west. This lane was described in 1820 as 'a road or way leading out of the Turnpike road to the village of Baldon'.

Two model cottages at the end of Rock Farm Lane. These houses, when built, had no ceilings to the bedrooms, and were divided by strong wooden partitions, open at the top, allowing air to circulate.

Church Street looking west. Church Street has recently been renamed Church Road but is known locally as 'along the Top'. The large house on the left is Elms Lea, built for the Rev E D Whitmarsh, vicar of Sandford 1877 to 1901, and was, at that time, the village vicarage.

Elms Lea, seen here c1902 with house servants Sarah Beckett and Edith Beecham, was bought in 1900 by George Clapperton, a paper manufacturer. The baby is D G Clapperton who became manager of Sandford Mill and was also cox for the Oxford boat race.

The main village shop, a bakery and grocer, in Church Street c1908. This remained very much the same until the 1950s when the frontage was altered. Mr Exon, the owner, is seen outside the shop, which, at this time was also the village post office and telegraph office.

Mr Exon, baker, delivered to Nuneham House, but was prevented from taking his delivery van through the main gates during the time of a visit by King Edward VII as it was thought that the motor vehicle could present a danger to the king.

A view of Church Street and the village shop c1950s from church tower.

A stone built cottage in Church Street, originally two stone cottages and a half timbered barn in one block. The cottage illustrated originally had a stone built bread oven on the front wall.

Cattle in Church Street c1960s.

Three farm cottages, converted from a barn sometime in 1890s. Known as Allins Cottages after John Allin, farmer at Temple Farm.

Roberts Row, seen here during the 1950s, lay at right angles to Church Street, behind the village shop. These six cottages were built c1830 and appear to have been a speculation by the village shop keeper of that time, Mr Roberts, to cash in on the expanding population brought in by the conversion of the flour mill to the manufacturer of paper by Mr Swan in 1826. The 1841 census shows the houses being occupied by a number of paper workers. The six cottages were converted c1890s into four-roomed houses by the addition of 'half a house' each end.

Mill Lane in the 1950s, leading to The Hades and the mill and river. Bassimore Farm House is on the left.

Bassimore Farm House, a 17th century building, from c1939 home of Dr Harold Edwin Hurst, Director General of the Physical Department for the Egyptian Ministry of Public Works from 1919 to 1946 and hence known as 'Hurst of the Nile'. Dr Hurst died in 1978, aged 98 years.

Fry's Barn, which formed part of the farmyard and out-buildings of Brassi-more Farm. It took its name from the Fry family, one member of which, Arthur, was in occupation by 1721. In 1851 Joseph Fry, then aged 80, was farming 196 acres at Tithe Farm, another name for Brassi-more Farm.

Mill Lane leading to the mill and Sandford Lock. Lined with fine oak trees, c1950s.

Mill Row was built by Mr Swan c1826 to house his first mill workers. These cottages were of exceptional design and far superior to most of the village cottages at that time, built with 'tarred' paper roofing. A second row of mill cottages was built in 1890.

The Red Houses on the London Road, built by Benfield & Loxley c1930s. Brick Kiln Lane is on the right-hand side, an earlier name being Clap-gate Lane. Note the ruts in the road made by the three engines delivering brick by road from the kilns. The first two houses were built for the brickworks manager and engineer, Mr Mills and Mr Rowles. This area used to be the site of the village pound.

Further along the London Road stood Sandford's first petrol pumps, installed about 1921 by Mr George Rowles. Mr Rowles had been the engineer at Benfield & Loxley brickworks and had also worked at the Oxfordshire Steam Plough Company in Cowley. The pumps stood outside his house which had originally belonged to the manager of the brickworks. The photograph shows Mrs Rowles c1927.

Nuneham Road in the 1930s. This road was also known as London Road, and later as Henley Road.

Herring's Shop, next to the Catherine Wheel on the London Road. In 1934 this was classed as a depot for omnibuses, run by Mr H Herring. He was known as a grocer, baker, butcher and 'pig sticker'. He was also a school manager and father to Ted Herring who later became the first headmaster at Northfield School.

The Fox Inn on the London Road c1930s, with Mr Charles Barrett, landlord, Mr H Benwell, and Sam the dog, standing in the doorway. Note the main road ran near the Inn frontage and did not allow a porch. The porch was built after 1931 when the new road had been cut through.

The Catherine Wheel in the 1930s.

The Catherine Wheel in the 1950s.

A group outside the Catherine Wheel in the 1930s includes C Beecham, T Reeve with dog, H Smith, Herbert Smith, Mrs Morris (publican's wife), W Morris (landlord), 'Potty' Smith, and Mr Crawford.

Temple Farm after a disastrous fire on 10 July 1994.

Church and School

An early drawing of St Andrews Church at Sandford before its reconstruction in the 1840s. This drawing is dated 1821 by J Buckler. Thomas Hearne, the local historian, had visited the church in 1745 and described it as 'a small thing, and of mean building'. Reproduced by permission of the British Museum.

View of the church from the south, c1894.

The interior of the church 1920s, showing the new pews which replaced the old box pews, new font and alter and pulpit also a new north aisle, all completed by the 1860s.

Sandford on Thames Benefit Society at their annual feast day assembly at the Club House, the Kings Arms Inn, c1890s. In the centre is the Rev Whitmarsh and on his right Mr Cannon, the paper mill owner, and on the left John Roberts, the secretary, with his short staff.

Founded in September 1858 as The Sandford Hand and Heart Benefit Society, but changed its name in the 1860s to The Sandford Independent Life Society, registered as Oxford 222. The organisation finished, after 60 years, in 1919, due mainly to the loss of members to Lloyd George's National Health Service. The annual feast day was held on the first Monday in July, with a feast held at the Kings Arms Inn. There was also a fair on the Kings Arms wharf which stretched up the village road as far as the mill cottages.

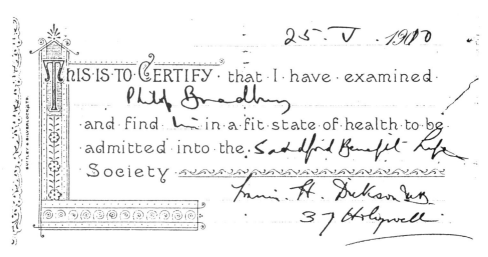

Before being admitted to the Society, a person had to prove that he was in good health. This certificate is for Philip Bradbury in 1900, possibly the same Philip Bradbury who was a labourer at the Sewage Farm.

Aerial photograph of 1929 shows, at the bottom, the earthworks in Church Close to the north west of the church. In earlier days these earthworks had been attributed to Oliver Cromwell's forces, but are now thought to be of a much earlier period, and either an ancient boundary ditch, or more likely the site of old Sandford village.

Thatched half timbered cottage that once stood on the corner of the London Road and Church Street. This picturesque building is said to have been a Dame School used by village children before the new village school was built in 1868. This picture is early 1900s, when the house was occupied by the Honey family.

School photo c1920. Left to right back row: Mrs Clark, ?, P Vaughn, A Hyde, S Langsbury, A Morris, ?, G Langsbury, W Smith, G Benwell, Middleton, G Seeney, ?, F Hyde. Third row: D Godfrey, C Taylor, A Hyde, Pitson, E Beecher, M Dodgeson. Second row: L Goldhawk, E Pitson, D Mills, M Cooper, C Smith, E Dean, ?. Front row: P Partridge, A White, R Reeve, D Webb.

School photo c1930s. Left to right back row: P Barrett, ?, T Dodgeson, B Godfrey, N Middleton, M Dodgeson, C Harris, D Gibbons, White, Miss Chaundy, W Clark, D Mills, D Marriot, E Reeve, G Harris, A Middleton, F Hyde. Front row: C Lansbury, G Taylor, B Attewell, ?, J Barrett, Pitson.

'Presentations to teachers: An interesting gathering was held at the Reading Room when Mrs Bolt, the headmistress of the school, who is resigning her appointment, was presented with a silver cake-stand and a salad bowl and server, subscribed for by former pupils and friends in the village. The Rev Latham said that Mrs Bolt had been governess of the schools for 21 years and seven months, and during all that time had only been absent for 13 days on one occasion when she was ill. Dr Sherwood a former vicar, wrote expressing regret at being unable to be present, and saying that when Mrs Bolt came to Sandford, the children were considered unteachable by H M Inspectors, but within two years the school was regarded as one of the best in that part of the county.'

School photo c1927 during the depression years. Left to right back row: T Smith, A Middleton, C Langsbury, E Reeve, G Harris, G Marriot, T Dodgeson, M Beecham. Front row: E Crickmay, P Marriot, ?, J Barrett, B Attewell, W Clark, S Tutty, G Taylor, L Harris, E Simms, G Harris, R Bostock.

In 1927 the village suffered an outbreak of scarlet fever, and children were sent to the Isolation Hospital in Marcham Road at Abingdon. This group includes Mrs Crickmay on the left, with A Middleton, Tom Smith and Ivy Dodgson.

The 19th century school house next to the church at Sandford.

Sandford Football team 1953–54 season. Left to right back row: Arthur Harris, W Kerod, J Tutty, ?, ?, ?, Albert Middleton. Front row: Cyril Middleton, John Bullock, Fred Druce, ?, ?.

Sandford Cricket Team c1950s. Left to right back row: George Clarke, J McClean, John Stone, Joe Smith, Les Gibbons, Cyril Middleton, Cecil Stone, ?, Albert Middleton, ?, H Vaughan, Ted Moore. Front row: C Becket, T? Dodgson, T Smith, P Dodgson, ?. Umpires L Gibbons and A Gibbons.

Employment

Sandford has always been a rural village and farming was an integral part of village life until the 1950s. There were many farms clustered around the village, and the parish of Sandford also included outlying farms to the east.

Temple Farm.

Picture fragment 1900s showing young calves grazing in the orchard. Note the fine gate and guards round the young apple trees, milk churns on the left. At this time Temple Farm was known as the Oxford University Experimental Farm.

Sandford paper mill from upstream, with the Kings Arms on the left, also known as Ferry Inn. Paper making commenced c1826, when the old corn mill was much altered by James Swan to undertake the manufacture of paper. The chimney shown is the second one and dates from around 1897.

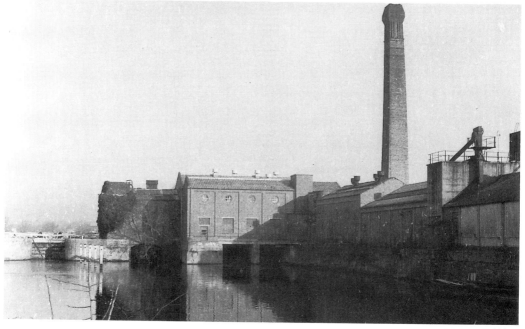

Cannon and Clapperton's paper mill from below, looking upstream c1960s. The new portion in the middle of the picture was built after a fire, one of many, which destroyed a great portion of the mill. The boiler house and stoke hole is on the extreme right and here can be seen the elevator for lifting the small coals to be pulverised before being fired under the boilers.

Frank Brookland emptying a beater with Michael Froud on the right. Beaten pulp is the raw material from which paper is made.

A group of mill workers c1929, includes W Naish, R Reeve, H Naish, F Smith.

Charles Pitson and Cliff Lansbury, who served over 100 years between them at the Paper Mill.

The paper mill yard with stocks of waste paper, as received, waiting to be processed, 1960s.

Mill yard seen here in the 1960s. The machine house is in the middle of the photograph, behind the sliding doors.

Staff outside the mill offices 1929. Left to right back row: C Pitson, M Gaskell, J Boughton, M Smith, W Naish, H Bostock, F Taylor, R Petch, C Pitson jnr., F Pitson, H Naish, R Gibbons, J Smith, A Whale?. Third row: E Naish, W Bullock, H Dodgson, H Clark, W Benwell, J Gaskell, A Gibbons, B Gaskell, L Gibbons, P Walton, W Taylor, T Naish, H White, R Reeve, O Tucker, W Partridge, H Dodgson, W Henderson (foreman). Second row: Petch, C Beecham, A Partridge, Dickenson, W Gardiner, A Tutty, J Middleton, J Nutt, Higgins, B Langsbury, White. Front row: E Naish, E Beecham, V Naish, C South, E Leach, M Tutty.

Benfield & Loxley brickworks started production in 1900 but ceased at the beginning of the first world war in 1914, their three engines going on to war service. The above, c1950, shows the remains of the site. The remaining chimney is that of the engine house, the kiln chimney being demolished in 1921 and the kilns removed.

In 1900 Benfield & Loxley bought land from the Manor to serve as a wharf for the delivery of coal for the kilns and delivery of bricks by barge via the river.

Pressed brick samples inscribed B&L Oxon.

One of Benfield & Loxley's three traction engines - a Wallis & Steevens. Mr Joe Middleton driver in the centre, photograph taken c1912.

Temple Farm c1940s.

Shepherd, Fred Elderfield, of Temple Farm and his flock c1926.

The first combine harvester to be used on Rock Farm. This is an early Allis–Chalmers four or five foot cut bagging combine harvester pulled by a Ferguson tractor. Dick Crabb is the driver and George Regan is bagging the grain on the combine.

An Oxfordshire wagon at Rock Farm in the 1950s. The wagon was said to be over a hundred years old when this picture was taken, and was thought to have been made by Sheldon of Wheatley

Lower Barn c1950.

Henry White, known as 'General', with lambs at Lower Barn, probably at the turn of the century.

Keeper's Cottage at Sandford Brake, to the east of the parish, was very isolated and had no services, note the bucket of water from the well. The last people to live in this gamekeeper's cottage were Mr and Mrs Fred Elderfield, seen here in the back garden, during the 1960s. Mrs Elderfield was taken ill in the great snow of 1963 and bulldozers were used to clear the way for an ambulance to rescue her.

Black Barn Cottage, seen here c1930 shortly before demolition, was a small isolated building on the large expanse of the Sewage Farm and was the home, for many years, of the Clack family. The term 'black' originates from the field name Black Molls and variations on this name.

Red Cottage c1960, now demolished, with Minchery Farm on the right. Standing as it did in an exposed position on the Sewage Farm, this worker's cottage had been struck by lightning many times, the repairs of which could always be seen by the new red roofing tiles. Occupied over the years by the Becket, Foster and Preston families.

Blackbird Leys farm house during the 1960s, when Mr Hodnett was in occupation. The name had originally been Black-Ford Leys, meaning the fields by the black ford, and the stream here was known as Black Brook.

Blackbird Leys Farm. This was occupied in 1851 by John Eglestone, farm steward of 413 acres, employing five servants. James Morrell bought the farm in 1857 and built new east and north ranges of farm buildings and enlarged the farmyard. In 1895 the Trustees of the Morrell estate sold Blackbird Leys and Sandford Brake farms to the City of Oxford. *'Blackbird Leys Farm was taken over by Mr Bishop during the 1920s. I remember his loads of fat pigs in a nice new wagon coming along Long Lane on their way to the Kidlington Bacon Factory, which was a new co-op venture by the Oxfordshire farmers.'* (Welch)

Saw Pit Farm, seen here during the 1960s shortly before it was demolished during the building of the Blackbird Leys housing estate. Saw Pit, together with Sandford Brake Farm and Blackbird Leys Farm were early 18th century settlements farming the eastern area of both Sandford and Littlemore parishes.

The River and Lock

The river has always been an important part of Sandford. The river and the locks have provided employment for many, together with the mill, which was the main source of employment for villagers. Surrounded as it is with water, it is not surprising that Sandford on Thames was often referred to as Wet Sandford, a reference, no doubt, to the frequent flooding of the village and surrounding land.

Ferry boat crossing the river loaded with a horse and Brougham carriage. Note the liveried men, evidently a person of some standing.

A fine view of Sandford Lock and the Mill c1880.

The toll bridge at the Kings Arms. Pedestrians were charged 1d and bicycles 2d. Regular toll taking was discontinued in the 1920s, but was always taken on Abingdon Fair Days, and probably ceased altogether in the 1950s.

Early view c1880s of Sandford Lock showing the grass-sided lock and original Lock House. Note the rack and pinion gate paddles. Stephen Blake, the lock keeper, was born in Abingdon. He died in 1902, having been at the lock for 34 years. Mr Blake was also a boat builder.

A house boat passing through the old grass-sided locks, probably on an outing to Nuneham Park, at the turn of the century.

Norman Clark, known as Nobby, lock keeper 1966–1984, on the old manual lock gear before modification to hydraulic opening.

The lock was rebuilt with hydraulic opening in 1966–67.

New lock and lock office c1972. Max Shefford was lock keeper at this time.

The Iron Bridge in 1972 before demolition, when the new cut was made. This bridge replaced an earlier wooden one in c1870.

Where the lasher stream rejoins the main stream below the lock, the bend had worn away on the Radley side, leaving a pool-like basin that became an excellent bathing place and was used extensively by the local population. During the hot summers of the 1920s and 30s Oxford buses brought large numbers of people out from Oxford to swim here, in what came to be called 'The Lido'. It became so popular that ice cream and shell fish vendors set up their stalls. Due to dredging in the 1950s, swimming at the Lido had been gradually abandoned. The Lido was finally filled in with spoils from a new cut and made further south in 1972.

Radley College boat house stood on the bend of the weir-stream where it joins the Lido. Radley College has had three various boat houses, and this photograph shows what appears to be the first of those buildings. A footpath ran across the fields from the college to this boat house. At this period the watermen would have been Mr Edwin Partridge, who was also a boat builder and lived in Sandford.

The eminent Victorian engineer, Sir John Hawksworth, reported on the river at Sandford in 1878 and described Sandford weirs and lock of this period. *'The channel to Sandford lasher leaves the river about half a mile above the lock. It is a wide channel now, but will require further increasing in width and depth, both above and below the lasher. The lasher is wholly insufficient in sectional area, and only 27 feet wide. It is closed by rimers? and hand paddles. There is an overfall weir of very rough construction adjoining, and there is another overfall weir between the lock channel and the river below the lasher'.*

Note the obelisk in the centre. This is believed to be far older than the inscriptions that currently appear on it. To whom or why it was erected has been lost in time, but it appears in an early drawing of 1821.

> To the Memory of Richard Phillimore and William Gaisford, students of Christ Church, who were drowned near this spot on the 23rd of June 1843.
>
> George William Manuel Dasent — junior student of Christ Church — drowned here on the 30th April 1872.
>
> Michael Llewelyn Davies, Ruper Erroll and Victor Buxton commoners of Christ Church, were drowned here on the 18th May 1921.

Henry Taunt's view of the small overflow weir in winter 1900.

The stream from the small weir to the main lasher stream. A popular place with cattle, but also with young boys, and called 'The Shallows'.

Aerial view of floods during 1959. Flooding was a regular occurrence in the area and major floods could stop production at the mill.

Anyone familiar with the area of Littlemore and Sandford will recognise the distinctive smells that sometimes pervade the area, particularly when the wind is in the 'right' direction, as recalled by an old Littlemore resident, Mr George Bampton in the 1960s. *'At this time the air was heavy with the revolting smell of sewage, and, if the prevailing wind or air current was blowing from a southerly direction, we, the residents, got the full impact of it. The field known as Spring Piece, from which Spring Lane possibly took its name, was one of the fields which used to be flooded and converted into a black evil smelling bog which encouraged flies and mosquitos in their thousands'.*

Following outbreaks of cholera in Oxford during the mid-1800s, the City Council formed a body known as The Local Board to provide an adequate sewage disposal system, After considering several sites, including Christ Church Meadow, the City of Oxford acquired upwards of a thousand acres of land in 1858, partly in Littlemore and partly in Sandford, for a sewage disposal farm. This was constructed in 1873 and enlarged in 1900. The method of disposal was known as open land treatment where crude sewage was allowed to flow through penstocks and furrows on to certain fields. The sewers from Oxford flowed down to a point near the end of Heyford Hill Lane, where a pumping station was built that lifted the sewage to a discharge point at the farm ground, ninety feet higher and some one and a half miles away.

All materials needed for construction were delivered either to Littlemore station and thence by horse and cart, or by narrow boat to a specially built canal about 100 yards from the river to the site. William Henry White was the Local Board's Engineer in charge of the work. The pumping station consisted of a pair of beam engines with the associated steam raising plant. The pump cylinders, having a diameter of 30 inches and a stroke length of six feet, moved 150 gallons per stroke, per pump at a rate of 14 strokes a minute. Pumping commenced in 1880 and the station was demolished in 1956.

Initially not all the land acquired for the Sewage Farm was needed, the remainder was let to tenant farmers at Great Leys, Blackbird Leys and Minchery. Sandford Brake Farm was retained to raise dray horses and as a holiday place and hospitalization for the cart horses used in the City.

Normal farm work was carried out on fields and banks which were being rested after flooding with sewage; corn, beans and vegetables were grown. A large number of workers were needed as most of the work was done by hand — during 1888, 36 men and boys plus women were employed, amongst them W Cordery (work on filter beds), E Titcombe (distributing sewage), A Clark (water to plough engine), A Rowland (attending stock), A Middleton (milking), H Beckett (keeping cows), J East (threshing beans), J Phipps (threshing beans), R Beckett (catching moles), W Smith (feeding stock at Littlemore), J Barton (sowing wheat by hand), Mrs Whiting (scaring birds), Mrs Barton and Mrs Cordery (picking squitch).

The Minchery
and
The Sewage Farm

The Benedictine Priory was founded by Robert de Sandford, one of the Knights of the Abbot of Abingdon, in the reign of King Stephen. The name of the Priory has varied between Sandford and Littlemore, but after the middle of the 13th century it was always known as the Littlemore Priory.

In 1220 Henry III paid 40 shillings a year for the upkeep of a boarder there and gave the nuns permission to collect firewood twice a day from his forest of Shotover. Thirty years later they were given 27 acres in what is now Open Brasenose for the same purpose. Records reveal that at an inquiry into the state of Shotover in 1363 the Prioress of Littlemore had cut down trees against the assize of the Forest.

It seems there were seven nuns living there in 1445 when it was visited by a Commissary of the Bishop of Lincoln, who reported they did not sleep in the dormitory for fear of it falling down. Two years later, a clerk of Oxford left them a small legacy to repair the house. At a later Visitation in June 1517 not only was the house in a shocking state but the lives of the nuns also. Both the Prioress and a nun had illegitimate children, property of the nunnery had been sold or pawned, nuns had been put in stocks for remonstrating with the Prioress and there was no money for food or to replace clothing. This report was followed by the sensational trial of the Prioress, Elizabeth Welles, in November of that year.

The Priory was dissolved in 1523 by Cardinal Wolsey.

The building later became known as The Minchery, from the word 'minchons', or nuns, and was the farmhouse for the Sewage Farm. When the engineers employed by the Local Board for laying out land for sewage disposal exposed in the farmyard a number of skeletons, some in stone coffins, of both sexes and different ages it was thought they were of people who had died in a poor house attached to the Priory. In the graves were many pavement tiles similar to those of Plantaganent times.

When farming ceased, the building remained empty until it was opened as The Minchery Farm Country Club, when a cow shed was renovated for use as a Night Club. Another change of tenant resulted in a change of name to The Minchery Tavern.

The Minchery c1905.

Anthony Yates was the farmer at The Minchery when it was visited by Thomas Herne in 1772, who stated that 'the Refectory was still standing though divided into more than one room. In it was a strange old table 13 feet 10 inches long and 2 feet 8 inches wide, nearly decayed, which was certainly the table at which the nuns used to dine. It was still used now and then at Harvest Homes and Sheep Shearings. Many coffins and bones have been found at the northern side of the house'.

The pond at Minchery Farm. Sam Bunce, a farmworker, was drowned in this pond while watering horses on Christmas Day 1927.

The Minchery at the turn of the century.

The Minchery c1950s, still surrounded by fine oak trees and retaining some of its previous splendour. The blacksmith's shop can be seen on the left.

Sewage farm workers, Phillip Bradbury on the left and foreman John Harris on the right c1920s

The Minchery was the farm house from where the operations for the sewage farm were directed and the activities included the breeding of horses for the farm work and also for the City. Around 1901 the Forge was constructed with red engineering bricks with no thought given to the fact that it was located between the stonework dairy attached to the house and the old stone barn. Harry Ede was the Bailiff and lived in the Minchery followed by his descendants whilst the old farming system continued – Les Ede was the last of the family to live there. A barn, called New Barn, stood in the fields near the Morrells bridge, as did a lodge house with its white painted gates and the remains of Sawpit Farm with its two cottages.

West view of the Engine House.

The Pumping Station in Heyford Hill Lane. Left to right: the Blacksmith's Shop, Coach House and Stable.

The houses of the Engineer and Assistant Engineer in Heyford Hill Lane, now privately owned.

Some of the machinery in the Engine House, which was demolished in 1957. Engineers in charge were Mr Milne from 1880, succeeded by William Anderson senior, who retired in 1920, William Anderson junior 1920–1934 and Sydney Page 1934–1956.

Pumping Station at Heyford Hill c1950, with Horace Feary, one of the engineers.

Workers at the pumping station c1950s. Left to right: Horace Smith, Mansell Titcombe, Harry Simmons, Tom Bradbury.

Aerial view of the Sewage Farm Pumping Station c1960.

By World War II the 1000 acres of the Sewage Farm had been reduced to 300 acres by lettings to tenant farmers and the land became overloaded, with sewage causing the persistent smells. James Campbell-Ridley, the City Engineer, made plans to deal with a flow of 5 million gallons of effluent per day from a population of 110,000, plus that from the factories, paper mills, breweries etc. In 1964 it was apparent an extension to the Works was needed to deal with an increase in the daily flow to 8 million gallons due to the expansion of housing development, industry, university extensions and hospital and an increase in water consumption. The extension, which had a capacity for treating 10 million gallons daily in dry weather and up to 40 million gallons in storms, was officially opened on Monday 6 Monday 1969.

In 1991 methane gas produced by sewage sludge was used to drive a generator supplying 670 kilowatts of electricity to customers of Southern Electricity.

SECTION TEN

War Years

ARP personnel of Littlemore and Sandford, outside Littlemore Village Hall. Left to right back row: ?, ?, ?, Michael Buckland, Jack Hudson, Horace Feary, James, Les Hudson. Middle row: ?, Druce, Hodgkinson, Bert Challice, Ellen Saunders, Bob Miller, ?, Sam Bunce, ?. Front row: Edith Feary, Bet Laitt, Aggie Crawford, Edie Kempson, Mrs Edie Tripp, Mrs Boughton, ?, Nina Nitycheryn, Miss Bunce.

Mrs Rivers, Women's
Land Army 1914–18
war.

Sandford village coach outing c1938. Left to right back row: Eric Naish, Gerald Naish, Mrs Naish, Mrs James, Barbara Evans, Mrs Crickmay, ?, Mrs Burnett, Mrs Winsor, Norman Reeve, Bill Boughton, Mrs Beecham, Nellie Brookland, Betty Attewell, John Stone. Front row: Mavis Pain, Michael Smith, John Smith, John Payne, Michael Naish, Tony Naish, Terence James, Audrey James, Christine James, Bob Crickmay with Geoff Crickmay in front, Bob Burnett, Ron Dean, Joyce Dean with David Winsor in front, Josey Boughton, Megan Winsor, Margaret Burnett, Hazel Attewell, Don Attewell, M Burnett (in bus doorway).

1945 celebrations in Newman Road, Littlemore. Mrs Haynes and daughter are seated in front, with Eleanor Saunders on left. Mrs Houlton is behind Mrs Haynes.

A welcome home party outside the old Reading Room at Sandford in 1945 for George Harris who was captured at Dunkirk while serving in the Oxon and Bucks regiment, and was a prisoner of war for five years in Stalag VIII.

The Reading Room. In the early days, the villagers had no public meeting place, other than the church, school and public houses. During the incumbency of the Rev Sherwood (1901 to 1910), the village purchased a second-hand portable building from the University, which had once stood outside the University Museum in Parks Road. This was drawn to the village by one of Benfield & Loxley's engines, and erected on a site where once stood three ancient earthen floored and thatched cottages. The Room was used during the 1939–45 war as headquarters for the Home Guard.

School Concert Party 1939. Front row: Mona Harris, Pete Benwell, Silvia Cook, Robert Crickmay, Joyce Neville, Alfred Neville (an evacuee). Note the criss-cross paper on the windows to help prevent injury from breaking glass should bombs fall.

Sandford Women's Institute coach outing c1930s, including Mrs Challenor sen., Mrs Stone, Mrs A Evans, Mrs Mumford, Mrs Hyde, Mrs Reeve, Mrs Stephens, Mrs Partridge, Mrs Morris, Mrs White, Mrs White sen., E Dobb?, Mrs Barrett.

Special Constables from both Littlemore and Sandford, pictured here outside the paper mill offices.

Littlemore Civil Defence.

Civil Defence, Sandford section. Left to right: P Winsor, S Cross, G Winsor, H Clark, V Cornish, Mrs Judd.

Sandford Home Guard. 4th Oxfordshire battalion No 2 company. Left to right back row: George Tutty, ?, Les Eade, Arthur Harris, N Pitson, ?, C Taylor, W Smith, F Birt, C Lansbury, J Leach, Messenger, G Cox, Kitchen, R Petch, L Wise, A Gibbons, Clarke. Middle row: F Petit, T Hagon, G Smith, C Stone, R Hyde, F Druce, N Reeve, Parker, J Bullock, H Vaughn, W Sheldon. Front row: J Birt, Sgr Davis, Mrs Parker (nurse), Bishop, Dorchester, F Reeve, F Clapperton, J Boughton, O Tucker, C Carter, S Buckler, Middleton, J Smith, F Birt.